THE
Wonder
Garden

WIDE EYED EDITIONS

22–29

THE **Chihuahuan Desert**

6–13

THE **Amazon Rain Forest**

WANDER THROUGH THE WONDER GARDEN AND EXPLORE FIVE EXTRAORDINARY HABITATS. HERE YOU WILL MEET REAL-LIFE ANIMALS IN FANTASTICAL ENVIRONMENTS THAT ARE INSPIRED BY NATURE.

30–37
THE **Black Forest**

38–45
THE **Himalayan Mountains**

14–21
THE **Great Barrier Reef**

STEP INSIDE THE
Wonder Garden

Beyond these gates, you will discover environments of astonishing diversity: the terrains, climates, and conditions here, and the challenges these pose to life, are each unique. But however different these habitats may seem, there is one thing that they share in common: each is an ecosystem made up of plants and animals that have found incredible ways to adapt and survive.

For many centuries, we humans lived on Earth in coexistence with nature, but today, more and more of us live a life apart, with the Wonder Garden on our doorstep left forgotten.

So, turn the page to creep through the **AMAZON'S** hot, humid rain forests, then dive down to discover the **GREAT BARRIER REEF'S** teeming shoals of fish. From there, travel to one of the driest environments on Earth, the **CHIHUAHUAN DESERT,** where horizons stretch endlessly ahead into the distance, and then, feel nature surround you on all sides as you wander into the faiy tale woodland of the **BLACK FOREST**. Lastly, travel to the roof of the world, the **HIMALAYAS,** from where you can see Earth's Wonder Garden roll out before you in all its majesty…

THE
AMAZON
RAIN FOREST

THE
Amazon
Rain Forest

UNEQUALED IN SIZE, COMPLEXITY, AND DIVERSITY, THIS RAIN FOREST IS THE WORLD'S ZOOLOGICAL JEWEL.

Dating back 55 million years, its scale is mind-boggling:
IT IS NEARLY 2 MILLION SQUARE MILES IN SIZE, AND PRODUCES 20 PERCENT OF THE WORLD'S OXYGEN.

*A*head of you is a dense, vast forest shrouded in mist. The air starts to thicken, the temperature rises, and the humidity makes you feel clammy and sticky. With every footstep, the foliage multiplies until it begins to dwarf you. The horizon becomes obscured by plants, and the sunlight that reaches the forest floor is dappled; you look up and see that you are shadowed by a giant canopy of trees that tower overhead.

Soon, you stand alone, swatting and swiping at insects, and listening to the howls and hoots of animals hidden in the undergrowth. You have arrived in the Amazon, the largest tropical rain forest and one of the richest concentrations of life on Earth.

Home to more than **5 MILLION SPECIES OF PLANTS, INSECTS, AND ANIMALS**, and over **1,500 OF THE WORLD'S BIRD SPECIES**, the vast size of this habitat is hard to imagine.

Carving through the rain forest's heart flows its spectacular life source, **THE AMAZON RIVER: MORE THAN 4,000 MILES LONG,** it contains more than 3,000 species of freshwater fish in its waterways and tributaries. Animals in this environment can cover vast territories, or rely on just one tree for their survival, but each, like its habitat, is extraordinary. Often, the animals are also extreme: the largest snake in the world, the green anaconda; one of the fiercest fish in the world, the piranha; and the lethally toxic poison dart frog all live here—and they may be just the tip of the iceberg, as **THERE ARE MANY MILLIONS THOUGHT TO BE LEFT UNDISCOVERED...**

RAIN FOREST

1. Black-headed
spider monkey *Ateles fusciceps*

2. Scarlet macaw *Ara macao*

3. Blue morpho butterfly *Morpho peleides*

4. Jaguar *Panthera onca*

5. Golden lion tamarin
Leontopithecus rosalia

Flight of Fancy

SOME OF THE AMAZON'S MOST SPECTACULAR SIGHTS ARE BROUGHT TO US BY THE BEAUTIFUL BIRDLIFE THAT FILLS ITS SKIES AND ADORNS ITS BRANCHES.

SCARLET MACAW
Ara macao

A FLASH OF RUBY AND GOLD FOLLOWED BY A PIERCING *SHRIEK!* announces the arrival of the scarlet macaw. Curious, social, and noisy, the macaw belongs to one of the most intelligent animal families on the planet: the parrots. These chatterboxes love company. They often mate for life, and group together in large flocks of up to 100 birds. But macaws aren't all talk: they are able to use tools and solve problems, too.

RED-BILLED TOUCAN
Ramphastos tucanus

***CROAK! CROAK!* CAN YOU HEAR THE CALL OF THE MAJESTIC RED-BILLED TOUCAN?** This is one of the largest of the 40 or so species of toucan in the world. It is a tree-dwelling bird, clumsy and heavy in flight, and happier to hop from branch to branch to seek out berries. Its huge bill is surprisingly light—made up of a honeycomb-like structure— and useful for reaching into nooks and crannies for food.

COLLARED INCA
Coeligena torquata

Close your eyes. Can you hear a humming sound? Look up, and if you see something hovering and darting in quick, jolty movements among the exotic flowers, you've spotted a collared inca, **A TINY AND DISTINCTIVELY MARKED HUMMINGBIRD.** The inca's wings, which it beats dozens of times a second, appear blurred to the human eye. Its heart pumps hundreds of times a minute in flight, and so the hummingbird relies on a high-energy diet of sugary nectar, which it extracts from flowers with its needlelike beak.

HARPY EAGLE
Harpia harpyja

Many animals in the rain forest, from the sloth to the spider monkey to the spiky porcupine, lives in fear of the terrifying harpy eagle, which soars at the top of the food chain with no predators of its own. **SHARP-BEAKED, LONG-TALONED, AND CROWNED WITH A CREST OF GRAY FEATHERS,** the harpy is the king of the Latin American raptors, and the largest—and most powerful—of all the eagle family. Nothing escapes its sharp eye; it spots its target, dives on its prey, and plucks it from the air with its huge, inescapable talons.

Life Abundant

BECAUSE OF ITS WARM, HUMID CLIMATE, AMPHIBIANS AND REPTILES ARE ABUNDANT IN THE RAIN FOREST. THE KIND THAT YOU COULD ENCOUNTER WILL DEPEND ON THE TIME OF DAY THAT YOU CHOOSE TO EXPLORE THE FOREST'S POOLS AND PLANT LIFE...

POISON-DART FROG
Dendrobates sp.

Poison-dart frogs may seem small and vulnerable, but they are able to freely wander through the forest by day because of the brilliant colours of their skin, which advertise to potential hunters that their bodies contain a **TOXIN SO LETHAL THAT AN ADULT HUMAN COULD BE KILLED** by eating one.

GLASS FROG
Family: Centrolene sp.

Wander out at night and you'll find that the forest has become a **CLAMOR OF MUSICAL CLICKS, WHOOPS, AND CROAKS.** Look up into the high leaves, where you will find the glass frog, calling out his high-pitched *PEEP!* which attracts female mates and warns other males away from his territory. Its skin belly is glasslike in its transparency—in some species you can see its heart beating!

BUTTERFLIES

Millions of migratory butterflies create a **WHIRLING CLOUD OF COLOR...** scarlet peacocks, blue morphos, and golden king swallowtails create a rainbow overhead.

GREEN ANACONDA
Eunectes murinus

SLOWLY WINDING THROUGH THE BRANCHES is the long, strong anaconda. This snake never stops growing, and becomes the largest in the world, killing its prey by wrapping it and crushing it to death.

BLACK CAIMAN
Melanosuchus niger

BEWARE THE BLACK CAIMAN stealthily sliding through the water. This creature is so powerful that fully grown—protected by its scaly armor and strong jaws—it becomes an apex predator, unhunted by any other species.

THE
GREAT
BARRIER
REEF

THE
Great Barrier Reef

THE WORLD'S LARGEST CORAL REEF SYSTEM IS SO VAST THAT IT CAN BE SEEN FROM OUTER SPACE.

But from close-up, it's even more amazing to look at:
RICHLY POPULATED WITH DIVERSE AND VIBRANT CREATURES, THIS IS THE LARGEST LIVING STRUCTURE ON EARTH.

Beneath your feet, the ground becomes sandy; a golden beach stretches out before you. There is a tang in the air, a salty breeze, and warm water laps at your feet. A boat carries you across the cobalt sea and stops to let you lower yourself into the warm and gently ebbing waters.

You dip your head beneath the surface and you are astounded by the riot of color that you encounter. Fluid sea grasses flow in the waters, and acid-colored fish dart and weave and pluck at the myriad of corals. Welcome to the world's biggest marine playground: the Great Barrier Reef.

Linking together **900 INDIVIDUAL ISLANDS ALONG A 1,400-MILE** stretch of Queensland, on Australia's coast, this is the biggest system of coral reefs on Earth.

Here you will encounter a dizzying array of wildlife: more than **1,500 SPECIES OF FISH, 30 SPECIES OF WHALE, DOLPHIN, AND PORPOISE, 600 KINDS OF CORAL, SIX SPECIES OF SEA TURTLE, AND 215 SPECIES OF BIRD** call this reef system home. But however vast it may be, it is under serious threat from pollution and climate change. When a coral is stressed by

changes in its environment, such as rising temperatures, it will expel the algae living in its tissue, which causes it to turn completely white. This is called coral bleaching, and it puts coral at a severe risk of dying. Here at the Great Barrier Reef, more than half of the coral has been lost in the last 30 years.

1. Clown triggerfish
Balistoides conspicillum

2. Giant cuttlefish *Sepia apama*

3. Common octopus *Octopus vulgaris*

4. Hermit crab
Dardanus deformis

5. Teardrop butterflyfish
Chaetodon unimaculatus

World of Color

A WORLD OF VIVID COLOR, INVISIBLE FROM ABOVE, REVEALS ITSELF BENEATH THE SURFACE OF THE WATER. HERE, IN THIS BEAUTIFUL BIOSPHERE, ORNATE FISH AND INTERLOCKING CORAL RELY ON ONE ANOTHER FOR SURVIVAL.

TUBE-DWELLING ANEMONE
Cerianthus sp.

With its tentacles waving gently as the waters ebb and flow, this tube-dwelling anemone is on the hunt. The alien-like creature partially buries itself into the seabed, and constructs a fibrous shell around itself, into which it retreats if it feels threatened. It reaches out its tentacles, which are coated with millions of tiny stinging cells, to paralyze and eat a passing victim.

SEA URCHIN
Heliocidaris erythrogramma

Small, nearly immobile, and totally unaggressive, one of the most painful encounters you could have in the coral reef is with a small spiny creature called a sea urchin. They are armored all over with long, defensive spikes as sharp as needles. It isn't just the urchin itself that benefits from its protective armor—small, defenseless fish take shelter there, too.

YELLOW-BANDED PIPEFISH
Dunckerocampus pessuliferus

This brightly colored relative of the sea horse has a long, snakelike body, which makes it a poor swimmer in open seas, but is perfectly adapted to the calm but crowded waters of the coral reef. It uses its long snout to pick off and eat small parasites on larger fish.

SPOTTED SEA STAR
Pentaceraster regulus

Search the seabed for a short while and you are sure to come across a starfish. As it ages, this species can change in color significantly, from blue to purple to black and gold. Protected with an armored top, with hundreds of tiny tube feet underneath, this animal has an amazing trick up its sleeve: it can regrow a lost limb.

THE GREAT BARRIER REEF IS
A POPULAR DESTINATION
FOR VISITORS, TOO.
EVERY YEAR, ITS
WARM AND SHELTERED
WATERS BECOME A NURSERY
TO WHALE CALVES AND NEWLY
HATCHED SEA TURTLES. DUGONGS, TOO,
ARE A COMMON SIGHT AS THEY
PASS THROUGH, SEARCHING FOR
SEA GRASS TO GRAZE ON.

DUGONG
Dugong dugon

Out toward the sandier shores,
gently grazing on the sea grass
meadows found in sheltered coastal
waters, you may see a dugong. This
slow, graceful beast—a cousin of the
elephant—is the only mammal in Australian waters to
live entirely on a vegetarian diet and travels vast distances
from one sea grass bed to the next in search of food.

GREEN TURTLE
Chelonia mydas

There are seven kinds of sea turtle in the world, and
six of them can be found here, in the Great Barrier Reef.
If you are lucky, you may see a green turtle, with its high-
domed shell and beaked mouth, which has returned from
the distant waters of Indonesia to the South Pacific to
nest and lay its eggs on the pristine sandy beaches.

Welcome Guests

DWARF MINKE WHALE
Balaenoptera acutorostrata

One of the highlights of your time in the Great Barrier Reef must surely be an encounter with a magnificent minke whale. Having gorged on krill in the Antarctic waters months before, the female minke whale travels north to give birth to her calf and brings it to the Great Barrier Reef during June and July to raise it in the tropical waters. This curious and friendly whale is well-known for seeking out human contact.

BANDED SEA KRAIT
Laticauda colubrina

You may encounter a smaller, but still memorable visitor: an inquisitive sea snake, which, although docile, has a highly venomous bite. Look for it at night, when it emerges to find food. If you see one, it's possible there are a lot more around, for they are known to hunt together, sometimes in the hundreds!

THE
CHIHUAHUAN DESERT

THE
Chihuahuan
Desert

SURVIVAL IS TOUGH IN THIS ARID REGION, WHERE TEMPERATURES SOAR, THEN PLUMMET BELOW FREEZING.

Straddling the border between America and Mexico, **THE CHIHUAHUAN DESERT IS ONE OF THE LARGEST IN NORTH AMERICA AND MAY BE THE MOST BIODIVERSE ON EARTH.**

*Y*ou find yourself climbing upward as the sun begins to set; your skin prickles as the temperature drops and your throat feels dry and parched as you breathe in the desert air. Before you unfolds a vast landscape with far-distant horizons and wide-open skies. Underfoot, the ground becomes scorched and scrubby, and strange, sculptural cacti emerge from the seemingly barren earth. They are abloom with flowers, turning the desert into a kalaeidoscope of color. Welcome to the Chihuahuan Desert: home to almost a quarter of the world's cactus species.

With a high altitude (averaging 4,000 feet), **TEMPERATURES HERE CAN FLUCTUATE WILDLY**, topping 110°F in summer, and frequently dropping below freezing in winter, when snowstorms are common. With such harsh conditions, it is hard to imagine how life survives here at all, but look closely and you will discover a rich and diverse ecology, with **MORE THAN 130 MAMMALS, 3,000 PLANT SPECIES, 500 BIRD SPECIES, AND 110 NATIVE FRESHWATER FISH.** And it's not just animals that have made this desert home, but many people, too. Today, grazing and overpopulation have put a strain on the desert's most precious resource— water. Rain is mostly blocked by two vast mountain ranges: the Sierra Madre Occidental to the west and the Sierra Madre Oriental to the east. Life, however, is supported by underground springs, which provide water, and of course the desert's life source, which flows through its heart: the **RIO GRANDE.**

1. Monarch butterfly *Danaus plexippus*
2. Mexican tiger moth *Notarctia proxima*
3. Bighorn sheep *Ovis canadensis*
4. Collared peccary *Pecari tajacu*
5. Black-tailed jackrabbit
Lepus californicus

Fight for Survival

HARSH CONDITIONS AND SCARCE FOOD SUPPLIES MAKE THE CHIHUAHUAN DESERT A DIFFICULT HABITAT TO SURVIVE IN. SPECIES HERE ARE TOUGHER THAN MOST, BUT NEVERTHELESS, SOME, LIKE THE MEXICAN WOLF, STAND ON THE BRINK OF EXTINCTION.

MEXICAN WOLF
Canis lupus baileyi

Just a few decades ago, the **HOWL!** of the Mexican wolf would fill the skies as the sun set over the desert. Today, they have been **HUNTED ALMOST TO EXTINCTION**, but a program is in place to bring the species back to the region. These social animals live together in packs with a complex hierarchy. They are excellent hunters, coming out at night when the sun has set, and working as a group to catch prey.

GREATER ROADRUNNER
Geococcyx californianus

Listen out for a **COO!** and a **CLATTER SOUND** to track down one of the most iconic animals from the Chihuahuan Desert: the roadrunner. As you might guess from its name, this bird prefers to cross the desert by foot, only taking flight if it feels threatened. Although its scurrying walk might look funny, the roadrunner is not to be messed with! With its strong feet and sharp bill, it **KILLS AND EATS VENOMOUS SNAKES**.

GOLDEN EAGLE
Aquila chrysaetos

Silently swooping across the skies, you might catch a glimpse of a golden eagle—the **LARGEST BIRD OF PREY** in the Chihuahuan Desert. As it soars overhead, it scans the scrubland for its prey—usually a small mammal, but sometimes as large as a coyote. Often it hunts with a partner: one chases its target until it is exhausted and finally makes way for the other to go in for the kill, **DIVING AT SPEEDS OF UP TO 200 MILES PER HOUR**.

JAGUAR
Panthera onca

The largest cat species in the Americas, the jaguar is another animal that was once a more familiar sight in the Chihuahuan Desert, but is now rarely seen prowling through the scrubland. This solitary hunter would emerge at dawn and dusk to track prey, but because it killed livestock, humans have now dramatically reduced its numbers.

Small World

MONARCH BUTTERFLY
Danaus plexippus

The monarch butterfly plays a crucial role in the desert's ecosystem. Every year, millions migrate through the desert en route to their winter home in central Mexico, and as they drink from the blooming flowers, they help to cross-pollinate the desert's varied cactus species.

BLACK-HEADED SNAKE
Tantilla wilcoxi

Gingerly lift up a small rock or log, and you might find a secretive black-headed snake beneath. This snake is small, reaching lengths of only 14 inches, and seldom seen, as it prefers to come out at night, when it can enjoy the heat of the ground without being scorched by the sun. While it may be small, it is also deadly—hunting and eating venomous scorpions.

DOWN ON THE DESERT
FLOOR, THE SPECIES ARE
NO LESS RESILIENT. MANY,
SUCH AS THE TERRIFYING TARANTULA,
ARE FEARSOME HUNTERS, WHILE
OTHERS HAVE FOUND
DEADLY WAYS TO DEFEND
THEMSELVES.

TARANTULA
Aphonopelma echinum

Scuttling across the ground at night, you
may encounter a large and hairy tarantula.
Instead of creating a web, this spider is
armed with a pair of venomous fangs with
which it injects venom into its prey.
But its appearance is worse than
its bite—it is relatively harmless
to humans, and
a bite from a
tarantula is no worse
than a bee sting.

MEXICAN TIGER MOTH
Notarctia proxima

Emerging from its cocoon in spring, the tiger
moth's brightly colored body and wings
advertise its foul taste to predators. Another
nocturnal creature, the tiger moth comes
out at night, when it emits ultrasonic
(high-frequency) sounds.

GILA MONSTER
Heloderma suspectum

The lumbering—but venomous—Gila monster
spends its summers hunting under the cover
of darkness, feeding on small rodents and birds.
It stores its fat in its tail,
which it relies on to survive
the harsh winter.

THE BLACK FOREST

THE
Black Forest

THIS DENSELY-WOODED MOUNTAIN REGION FORMS A 100-MILE STRIP IN SOUTHWESTERN GERMANY.

Home to the elusive lynx and, reputedly, the unicorn, **THIS ANCIENT, ENIGMATIC FOREST IS IN A CORNER OF THE GLOBE WHERE THE BOUNDARIES BETWEEN FACT AND FICTION BLUR.**

Trees spring up around you as your journey takes you into the heart of a mysterious, dark forest. The crack and rustle of your footsteps hushes the wildlife all around, but when you stop to listen, a chorus of animal sounds fills the forest air. The dense woodland gives way to a meadow, flooded with wildflowers in spring and blanketed by snow in winter, but now, in summer, a vision in green. You cross this open space, trailing your hands through the high grasses, and the soft roar of water is brought to you on the breeze. Following the sound, you discover a thunderous waterfall carving its way down the valley.

This mountainous region of southwestern Germany, bordered by the Rhine Valley to the south and west, is one of the world's most ancient woodlands. Today it covers almost **4,000 SQUARE MILES**, but this is just a fraction of the vast area it spanned many centuries ago. First called the Black Forest by the Romans, this region is so-named after the **DARK-COLORED PINES** that once grew so densely in places that the forest was almost impenetrable to humans. Walking its wooded pathways today, it is easy to understand how this romantic landscape of snowy peaks, waterfalls, fairy rings, bogs, and moss-covered glens became the backdrop to some of Europe's most popular and enduring fairy tales, including *Rapunzel*, *Snow White*, and *Hansel and Gretel*. The lush, green landscape is interspersed with **MANY MOUNTAINS, EIGHT RIVERS** (including the Danube), and **SEVERAL HOT SPRINGS**, making it a rich habitat that supports a diverse range of flora and fauna.

1

2

1. Eurasian lynx *Lynx lynx*
2. Red fox *Vulpes vulpes*
3. Great spotted woodpecker
   Dendrocopos major
4. Eurasian badger *Meles meles*
5. Eurasian red squirrel *Sciurus vulgaris*

High and Mighty

IT WON'T TAKE YOU LONG TO DISCOVER THAT THE BLACK FOREST IS A HAVEN FOR BIRDS— JUST CLOSE YOUR EYES AND LISTEN...

COMMON KINGFISHER
Alcedo atthis

Head to the riverbank, and if you catch a flash of copper and cobalt, it could be a kingfisher, **DARTING AND DIVING** in search of a meal. Relying on a diet of fish (and other water-based creatures), its eyes are specially adapted to reduce the reflected light on the water's surface, which allows it to spot its prey beneath—and helps it see clearly underwater, too.

EURASIAN EAGLE-OWL
Bubo bubo

Pause to listen—the deep **OOH-HU** that resonates through the forest, followed by a rasping **KVECK–KVECK!** sound, is the call of the eagle-owl. This mighty hunter—one of the **LARGEST KINDS OF OWL ON EARTH**—surveys the forest floor from a branch, waiting to spy its prey below. Once its target comes into sight, it swoops down on it and snatches it with its strong talons.

COMMON RAVEN
Corvus corax

An unmusical **PRRUK-PRRUK-PRRUK** noise announces the presence of the raven. If you detect a sense of curiosity in its gaze, you are right—this bird has been found to be **A CREATURE OF REMARKABLE INTELLIGENCE**. This crafty and playful animal has excellent problem-solving abilities, and has an eye for round and shiny objects, such as pebbles or pieces of metal, which it steals and hoards away to impress other ravens.

Floor of the Forest

EUROPEAN ROE DEER
Capreolus capreolus

You could be confused for a moment by a doglike **BARK!** sound, which actually belongs to the diminutive roe deer. In medieval times, this species was abundant across Europe, but later, in the 19th and 20th centuries, hunting reduced its range and numbers. **WELL-CAMOUFLAGED IN WOODLAND**, you are most likely to spot one in the forest's grassy clearings.

WANDER OFF THE PATHWAY AND YOU WILL FIND YOURSELF IN A FAIRY TALE–LIKE FOREST OF TIMES PAST, WHERE RED DEER ROAM FREELY AND WILD BOAR SNUFFLE ACROSS THE FOREST FLOOR.

RED DEER
Cervus elaphus

The **ROAR!** that echoes through the forest is the sound of the red deer—a social animal that lives in large herds during the summer. The approach of autumn is a dangerous time for the dominant stag, who must **FIGHT TO PROTECT HIS HAREM OF FEMALES** and defend his territory from other males.

WILD BOAR
Sus scrofa

GRUNTING its way through the undergrowth, you might meet a wild boar. Famous for its versatile diet, you are most likely to find this creature rooting for food on the forest floor—and no wonder: a fully-grown boar needs to consume around **TWICE THE CALORIES** per day than the average adult human.

THE
HIMALAYAN
MOUNTAINS

THE Himalayan Mountains

SNOWCAPPED PEAKS AND LUSH VALLEYS BRING A SAVAGE BEAUTY TO THE ROOF OF THE WORLD.

Home to Everest, the highest mountain on Earth, **THIS MOUNTAIN SYSTEM LINKS MORE THAN 100 PEAKS THAT STAND HIGHER THAN 24,000 FEET ABOVE SEA LEVEL.**

Your final journey takes you through a bamboo forest, and as you climb, the temperature drops and the winds rise, burning your cheeks and numbing your fingers. Clouds scud across the sky forming a dark gray mass overhead and suddenly your vision is blurred by a flurry of snow. The storm passes, but now your feet are sinking knee–deep in snow as you walk. You begin to pant because here you are up so high that the air is thinner. Finally, you turn around to see how far you have come and a magnificent mountainscape sweeps before you. You are standing at the top of the world, on the mighty Himalayas.

Stretching 1,550 miles from east to west and covering a total area of 230,000 square miles in Southern Asia, the Himalayas aren't only home to the highest peaks in the world, but also some of the largest glaciers. Despite its massive size, it is one of the youngest mountain ranges on Earth, and is, in fact, still rising at a rate of 5 millimeters each year. Named after the Sanskrit words, "hima" for "snow" and "alaya" for "abode," the Himalayan climate is perhaps best-known for its snowstorms and high winds, but conditions here are changeable and treacherous in all kinds of ways, depending on the height above sea level: monsoons, floods and landslides, earthquakes and tremors are also common dangers in different regions. This means that the wildlife and variety of species that have adapted to survive here can vary enormously, from the tropical forests in the foothills, to the barren, rocky mountainsides.

MOUNTAIN

1. Himalayan woodpecker
Dendrocopos himalayensis

2. Crested hawk eagle *Nisaetus cirrhatus*

3. Black-necked crane *Grus nigricollis*

4. Himalayan monal pheasant
Lophophorus impejanus

5. Demoiselle crane
Anthropoides virgo

Life in the Foothills

ASIATIC BLACK BEAR
Ursus thibetanus

As the worst of the cold weather passes, you may hear a noisy—and grumpy!—asiatic black bear, or moon bear, emerging from its den, where it spent the **WINTER MONTHS IN HIBERNATION**. This species is easy to spot thanks to the V-shaped pale flash of fur on its chest. A night-time hunter, it spends much of the day asleep.

THE HIMALAYAS MIGHT BE BEST KNOWN FOR THEIR SNOWCAPPED PEAKS, BUT DESCEND TO THE FOOTHILLS OF THE EASTERN SLOPES AND YOU'LL FIND BAMBOO FORESTS BLANKETING THE RUGGED TERRAIN.

BENGAL TIGER
Panthera tigris tigris

Sit still and hold your breath as you see a ghostly creature step out of the shadows: a white tiger patrols the grasslands, looking for its next kill. This **SNOW-COLORED HUNTER** is the offspring of a Bengal tiger—a rare mutation in its genes has caused its amber fur to fade to an unearthly white. The Bengal tiger's numbers have dropped dramatically in recent years due to habitat loss and poaching.

RED PANDA
Ailurus fulgens

Curled up in a tree with its tail over its eyes all morning, you might hear a red panda waking up in the afternoon, uttering **TWITTERS** and **TWEETS**. Relying on a gentler climate for its survival, it can be found in the temperate forests of the Himalayas. It is a little larger than a domestic cat, and is an excellent climber, but it is ungainly and waddles on land because of its short front legs.

Higher Ground

AS YOU CLIMB HIGHER, THE MOUNTAIN SHRUGS OFF ITS THICK FOREST CLOAK. BUT THIS ROCKY REGION ISN'T DEVOID OF LIFE: IN SPRING AND SUMMERS THESE MOUNTAIN MEADOWS ARE ABLOOM WITH FLOWERS, AND SOME SPECIES, LIKE THE SNOW LEOPARD AND HIMALAYAN GORAL, ARE TEMPTED TO VENTURE UP ABOVE THE TREE LINE.

SNOW LEOPARD
Panthera uncia

This endangered species—a hunter, and **MASTER OF STEALTH**—is even more difficult to find in the wild than its prey, the goral. Its thick, patterned gray fur blends in with the snow-covered rocks and allows it to creep up on its victim, before chasing it down steep slopes and pouncing on it from above.

HIMALAYAN GORAL
Naemorhedus goral

Quick and nimble-footed on the rocky terrain, you might find it tricky to spot the wary goral, which is **PERFECTLY CAMOUFLAGED TO BLEND IN** with its rugged surroundings and is mostly active during the dim light of the mornings and evenings. It lazes in the sun through the daytime, only making its characteristic **SNEEZE!** sound if threatened.

YAK
Bos mutus

Another animal you might catch a glimpse of is the yak—the largest animal in this region. Many domesticated yaks are kept by herders, but there is a **SMALL POPULATION OF ITS WILD COUSIN** still living in the Himalayas, too. Covered from head to hoof in a dense woolly coat, it is perfecty suited to the harsh conditions of the mountain.

Index

Imprint

For Eiðar and Ísól, my two squirrels, and with thanks to Joanna Bagge, whose work on this book has helped make it what it is today

WIDE EYED EDITIONS
www.wideeyededitions.com

Written by Jenny Broom

First published in the United States in 2015 by
Wide Eyed Editions, an imprint of Quarto Inc.,
276 Fifth Avenue, Suite 206, New York, NY 10001.

ISBN 978-1-84780-703-8

The illustrations were created digitally
Set in Avenir, Bebas Neue, and Mrs Eaves

Layout design and typography by Sinem Erkas
Conceived and commissioned by Rachel Williams
Created in consultation with Dr. David Gower and
Filipa Sampaio at the Department of Life Sciences,
The Natural History Museum

Printed in Dongguan, Guangdong, China

9 8 7 6 5 4 3

KRISTJANA S WILLIAMS studied graphic design and illustration at Central St. Martins. She won critical acclaim during her eight years as Creative Director of Beyond the Valley and 2013 saw the studio Highly Commended for Best Use of Colour at the Dulux Let's Colour Awards. Subsequent awards include the D&AD Award, a New York Festivals Grand Prix and First Prize, a prestigious CLIO Award, and short-listing for the Cannes Lions Award. Born in Iceland, she lives and works in London.

JENNY BROOM studied at the Slade before becoming an author and editor of children's books. Her natural history title *Animalium* was voted Children's Book of the Year by the *Sunday Times*, and short-listed for the National Book Awards and Blue Peter Award. She lives and works in London

To Find Out More...

Animal Diversity Web
An online database of animal natural history provided by the University of Michigan's Museum of Zoology.
www.animaldiversity.org

BBC Nature: Habitats
An online collection of habitats from around the world.
www.bbc.co.uk/nature/habitats

National Geographic
Be inspired to care for your planet with this resource provided by the National Geographic Society.
www.nationalgeographic.com

Natural History
This book, authenticated by the Smithsonian Institution's National Museum of Natural History, contains information on more than 6,000 species. DK Publishing 2010

WWF
Explore diverse habitats from around the globe with this conservation charity's website.
www.worldwildlife.org/places